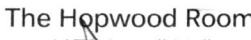

Santorini Poems

To Hopwood with love —
upon Santorini Jubilee,
Rebecca, it is
magic!

10.10.X.19

Santorini Poems

by
John Karabetsos

Copyright © 1994 by John Karabetsos

ALL RIGHTS RESERVED. No part of this publication may be reproduced, distributed, or transmitted in any form or by any means, including photocopying, recording, digital scanning, or other electronic or mechanical methods, without the prior written permission of the publisher, except in the case of brief quotations embodied in critical reviews and certain other noncommercial uses permitted by copyright law.

    For permission requests, please address
    Thalassa Press
    3057 W. Lyndale St.
    Chicago, Il 60647, USA

Published 1994 by Thalassa Press
Printed in the United States of America

Photography by John Karabetsos
Cover Illustration, Nea Kameni 2

22 21 20 19   1 2 3 4

ISBN 978-0-692-17785-3
Library of Congress Control Number: 2018910426

Goddess daughter of Zeus,
Sing in me, O Muse,
Beginning at whatever point you will...

—Homer

Table of Contents

Section		Page
	Foreword	xi
I	Corinthian Soliloquy	5
	he rows standing up	6
	I float like driftwood	7
	one one thousand two	8
	Olive Grove	9
II	Mortal Leaf	13
	her eye in profile	14
	diver from the rocks	15
	four legged bed frame	16
	Mother of Nine Muses	17
III	Take the Moon from the Glass	23
	we lay on couches	24
	shapely drinking cup	25
	the baker's wine shop	26
	Murder at the Drive-In	27
IV	Ambassadors	31
	passing the old field	32
	lamp above the door	33
	tat tapping typebars	34
	Zeus the Hospitable	35

V	The Keeper and the Garden	39
	two abandon dogs	40
	komboloi for sale	41
	coffee grounds settle	42
	Mosquitoes in Your Ear	43
VI	Danced and Jested	49
	the cigarette girl	50
	five needles cluster	51
	white spruce stands alone	52
	Wind to a Sail	53
VII	Lost in Translation	57
	a carpenter thinks	58
	we've spent our lifetime	59
	life's precious colour	60
	Balconies	61
	About the Author	71

Illustrations *Facing Pages*

Nea Kameni	2
The Human Condition	10
City Dionysia	20
Temple of Zeus	28
Torso	36
Port of Call	46
Venenzia	54

End Matter	*Facing Pages*
Nea Kameni 2	64
Ancient Thera	66
Thera	68
Author	72

Foreword

In 401 B.C. after the disastrous battle of Cunaxa in Babylon, the reluctant leader Xenophon shepherded his beleaguered army through hostile Mesopotamia, Kurdistan and Armenia. Ultimately this "marching republic" reached the shores of the Euxine Sea which they greeted with their famous exultant cry "thalassa, thalassa!" (the sea, the sea!). It meant their beloved Aegean to the west was within their battered embrace: relief, rest, rejuvenation.

When the reader encounters these remarkable Santorini Poems he embarks on a journey—challenging, arduous but in the end intensely and immensely rewarding. John Karabetsos bathes us in blue Ionian waters. He asks us to sweat, to smell, to revel in the heat, the blinding white sun filled sensations so convincingly caught.

There is Myth here as well as a modern poetic bridge spanning the centuries. It's a strong structure, a steely discipline encouraging the reader to climb truly Parnassian heights.

Careful engagement with these poems will result in the same exaltation and exhilaration that rose from the throats of Xenophon's army all those years ago.

—by Daniel Reardon

I.

Corinthian Soliloquy

the unsleeping embrace
encoils with dragon flesh and spite
this spurred Colchian chase
relents not its seductive plight

with hours do hours onslaught
by lake sea stream 'til threshold brink
might I ease weary thought
and into the unconscious sink

beneath glory beams cast
the brails 'bout spar and sail that bask
ashore the unstepped mast
o'er sand waves grope tempt'ng fates at task

O Hypnos lull those shades that'll let me drift
among twilight mist as a lion dreams
his sense of nape reared his shoulder blades shift
what bronze footstep what oak bough so gnarled gleams
tall dry grass somnolent chimes of straw
in Night's belly salt wings so nestle awe
with no past and no present I rest here for now
like a poppy is red put the breeze to my brow

he rows standing up
fisherman beyond the cove
lee side of the isle

I float like driftwood
the calm surf doesn't seem to mind
windmills are sleeping

one one thousand two
counting the lighthouse turn
two one thousand three

Olive Grove

whosoever should remember
certain words have colour
to blush is the sound of plums
bleeding garlic smells of honeymoon

who so forthwith would give mind
to marvel the slow afternoon
recall then this olive grove
and bid providence finds you there

visited among torsos a thousand years thick
wide crowns whose timid fleshy drupes dangle
coupled and clustered about elliptic leaf
volumes of slender blade gathering light
all rustling together the greens
those dusty those indirectly lit
the verdant backsides almost silver
tinsel flitting its tendency toward white
olive trees along flat along gentle slope
illuminant natures bulk overhead
the humble ground cover listens
grasshoppers drone upon dry wind

II.

Mortal Leaf

autumnal brace in e'en belated hour
betraying leave unto the baiting mire
what last gasp bides before this bog devour
a leaf's will to wield its body entire
exultant speed felt through inside and freed
where to some travler's eye opaquely glares
alas discerning sense among the reed
how this feast of souls in radiance dares
an aureole choir of undulant sway
unbosomed brilliance pinnately imbued
ol' ochros laughs now the abscission lay
sweet sanguine lips welcome earth's fortitude

leave a glass for the dead aside the sash
outside there's burnt umber under white ash

her eye in profile
the trust in meeting like this
new light sheds itself

diver from the rocks
arms stretched out over the sea
honey drops so long

four legged bed frame
can you recall all those smells
crushed linen gathers

Mother of Nine Muses

kind Memory
come serve the events of Night's past
sacred ways back
to collect again ourselves
from where we were
the cafés, the tavernas, markets
from volcano dust
titaness mother
we were songs, egyptian sand

Theophilos
issued from the bone yard
of simple engines
his dusty lot and knotted grey tufts
wrung out with oil
the unbreakable comb
he's ready for drinking

after falls the lonely streetlamp
bottle cap backgammon plays itself out
astride the narrow cobbled path
a bellowed rasp summoned
Theophilos waving his desire
with pointed finger
like a rock a vulture a chain a-roving
befit compassion wore down his sleeve
and oxtailed about his tongue
what to do with the big ouzo

[continued on next page]

[Mother of Nine Muses, cont.]

yet soon did blue monkeys come at play
conducting directly his reason away
his liver short of breath and looted fancy
imparting unto fallen attendants limp and limb
a mangled eloquence to approximate
some balance of history

these island roads are too small
one morning I'm going to get hit by a bus
on a wrong step
in a hangover

III.

Take the Moon from the Glass

alas above the open sea—testimony
we've waited haven't we, resting 'til now our desires
beside water line like a slow drawn willow tree
my certain faith called to light by distant spun fires
she wheels before the steep black her worldly climb
and I watch crouching under this frame colossus
her promise burns past hulking mountain backs of time
my bringer of knowledge my Moonlight unashamed
yes enchanted hillside pitched on the village edge
how well your sturdy roof knows these restless dice
each lapsing night in hope of her sole privilege
sweet Selene her life blood sown with milky spice
curiosity gives way, there's want in your thigh
—come pull back that nocturnal fabric grown ripe
we'll draw the ecstasy of our ancestors nigh
distilling angelica root from reed and pipe
coriander song in a trembling anise drop
exuding sweat and pressed skin born here twice again
tell me Selene where does necessity stop
tonight, beyond the lustral basin dare we pass
and drink of Eros from the glass

we lay on couches
after evening meal again
watching acrobats

shapely drinking cup
god's vessel of fragrant games
we share five senses

the baker's wine shop
underneath Thera's stone square
warm belly of fire

Murder at the Drive-In

god we got drunk
our drinking it is what it is
each naked face under the stars

I turned up the volume
through the window
and so did they

IV.

Ambassadors

always another city down the line
corrupting expectations we once knew
to sing our mysteries mixing wine

companions we were flotsam on the brine
philagoric spirits a driving crew
always another city down the line

secret sharers dancing by the moonshine
exchanging courtyard faith in twilight's blue
to sing our mysteries mixing wine

if transcendent sky and earth be entwine
then let wild skins drape the shoulders of issue
always another city down the line

somewhere Atlas weeps for his own friendless shrine
blessëd grounds we reinvented anew
to sing our mysteries mixing wine

mark well the dying act of Constantine
a vague intimation through the foggy dew
always another city down the line
to sing our mysteries mixing wine

passing the old field
crickets and a ruined wall
revelers at night

lamp above the door
prophylactic on flower
shades of yellow light

tat tapping typebars
two keys jam a moment's pause
anticipation

Zeus the Hospitable

my sifted charts and blotted symbols
in quarters standing by
on a line with no finite edge
haphazard dreams collide
crossing lightly this glass twilight
sax tones invited a change in air pressure
take me blustery tongue where you will

out to sea from the city
there where we meet
midst primal water
inestimable Sky
Sky the overseer
unto a subject Sun
claimed this correct order
was the natural aim for now

wine stains hem the puss
under winking testicles
Kostas laughed
yes—just a man
lingered in this lagoon of stars
with white hair braided to Night's strand
his fist shook the table
a scavenge beetle crushed

there is justice
with the animal in its cage

V.

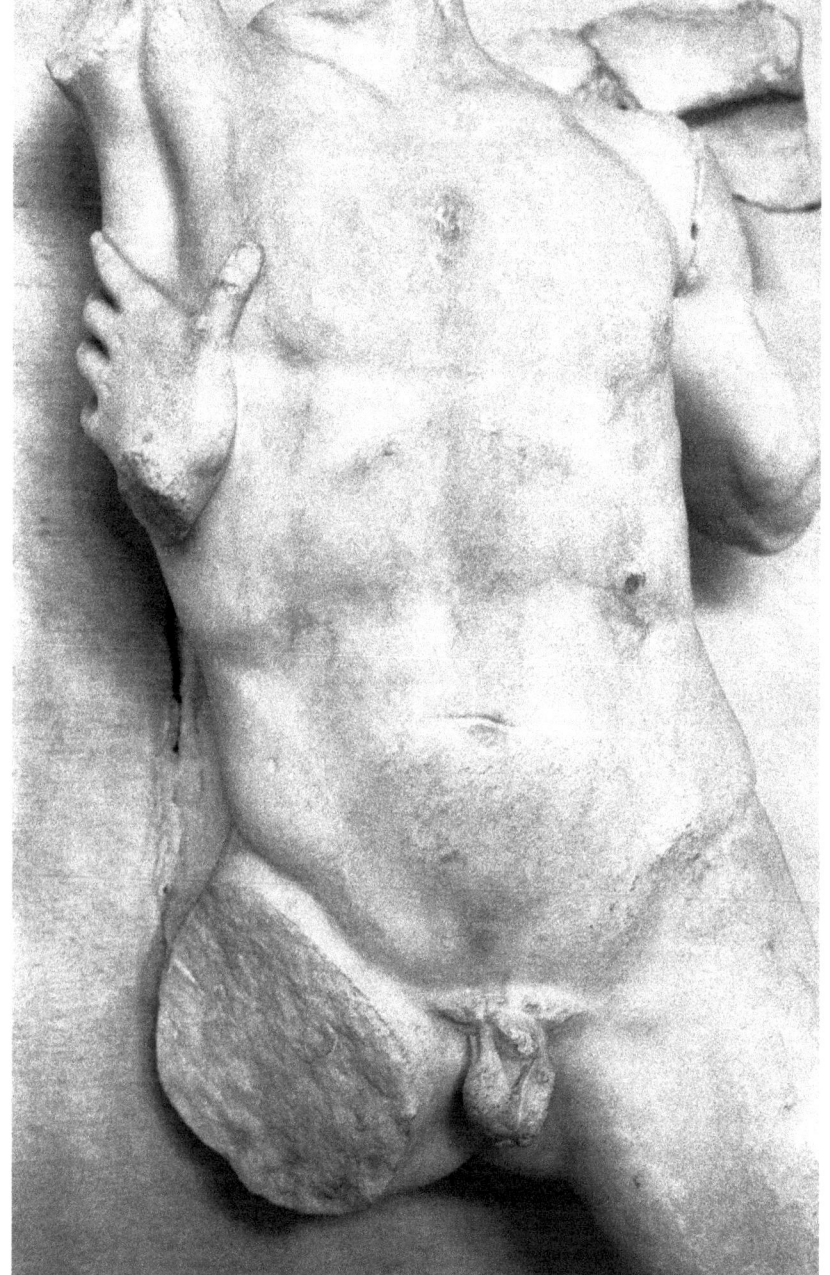

The Keeper and the Garden

and so enters a little sound alee
off lying branchlets are boasting their height
partake the hydrous veins of azurite
allay your flowered thirst with all you see
this lowland glade is paradise set free
proclaiming creation's earthly birthright
where faunal hordes envelop oiled delight
the wellsprings plash and garnish humming bee
entreat you I meanderer as grim
I keeper to cradle song everlast
with teeth two pennies long 'n thin blade aloft
sun blistered white my ogled sight's gone dim
strawberries know I for their scent damn blast
your step in the cool of the day go soft

two abandon dogs
with a nose for business
humping in the street

komboloi for sale
blue beads on their shiny chain
my soul is a fish

coffee grounds settle
our separate destinies
small cup turned over

Mosquitoes in Your Ear

I sit
sweat and walled in
this room
counting remains of the ones
slapped against the cool paint
most are smeared in blood they have stolen
I can't sleep
in my nakedness I'll have a cigarette
and wait they will come
buzzing growing in closeness
stops
or fades away unseen
like women of the night
like silence disturbed
the buzzing in my ear I hear them
they want me to move
coaxing
draining me little by little
to play the game
I can't win and if I start
it doesn't matter
kill one and another
there will always be mosquitoes
beside my ear
whispering
fill out this form
sign here
and we're all set

[continued on next page]

[*Mosquitoes in Your Ear, cont.*]

from across the room I can see
the smoothness of her upper thigh
among the wrinkled sheets sleeping
but I won't go back to bed
ever again

VI.

Danced and Jested

I've played the fool a jangled frolic muse
who'll leap infused with light from selfless stage
abusing fashion's fruit beneath laced hues
a fallen satyr seducing outrage
against the fate who serves this wayward age
inclined to fancy if we ev'r were born
fray tapestries in the wings of Night's page
all destine souls before that titan morn
where dignity's sheep are led to be shorn
my phantasmal lengths strap solitude's pole
allurëd Mephistophelian horn
all thralldom gained by an agoring toll
I've played the fool which was the tragic role
and comic does seem there after

the cigarette girl
redolent sticky resin
among balsam fir

five needles cluster
pubescent twig this year's whorl
two centuries tall

white spruce stands alone
a woodsman stopped and was moved
sturdy unkempt tree

Wind to a Sail

sixteen fifty-three New Amsterdam
Peter Stuyvesant governs trade
hostage children for beaver pelt
twenty-five tobacco sticks
leaves beat the chest of their felled trees
those racked bones of the barricade
across Wall Street soon York will receive
red wampum golden seed

celestial bodies set forth
east bound for eternity
meaning everything and nothing
on a paper page

VII.

Lost in Translation

the rib-cage shows below the breasts
and above the panting belly arching sensation into night
blood bright of Haemon's last breath rests
upon white cheeks sealing an enfolding embrace
beyond a tomb's depths
the throttle riding hard hails wind
to chant howled rhythms in drunken ears there is no light
on this road only fireflies pulling you further into night
a monk to icon fate akin told me once he believes in miracles
as life is   as we walk
a poem rising to lips spoke of God   an almond tree blossom

the best loved cigarettes are five
with black coffee first thing after sleep
                              another after sex into night
elusive smoke that pours from fire of lilacs
that sprinkle sunset contours a hand's skin in Pythian dance
                            the kiss
                    poetry is something lost in translation

sensation arching back in bed
lays better torn in sheets unsaid
the body as the night's despot
translated is what it is not
futilitarian abyss
the mouth in fetters words a hiss
so lets not speak of this the kiss
but only feel it savage in the heart

a carpenter thinks
the span of a wooden beam
how long will it last

we've spent our lifetime
in the storeroom counting jars
building an empire

life's precious colour
painted nails disheveled hair
bleeding from the foot

Balconies

how is it you saw the sunset
a cafe terrace over Fira's depth face cliffs
along that wall repose where we had once met lips
through darkened myth a lighthouse spurred respiring veins
or Oia's vanishing ferry glimpse where calm ordains
and I in sombre thought across sprawling waves
Aegean bound this wake it steals those nights like knaves
those powerful cleft memories a Doric sea
    Santorini

how is it you saw the sunset
from carnious step edge
both ends that burn a cigarette
combust the paths through tulles
to lurid fathoms kedge
hearth choral pulses beset
in frieze iambic schools
are prismatic allied
which night was it we shared a drag
exhaling dolphinia mist
adyta archëd tide
the sound of legs entwined brush free
lain poise in gloria

[continued on next page]

[*Balconies, cont.*]

how is it you saw the sunset
untamed fain voices veil
to winded skin the Phoebus temp
down body's switchbacks sped
the soul hoist ready sail
for horses rile the calm exempt
unanchored storms we'll tread
as in a movie I once saw
he said— there can be more than one
            ending in a lifetime
a gull hovers in lungs of the sky
unseen against whitewash houses
spattered amongst the swift face of land
passing and I wonder

how is it you saw the moon
what truth you sought that lurks in Loxian night breath
on nature's cliffèd portico by Nazareth
god bleeding earthquakes screaming through the mouth
holding back suffocated by constellations
            said nothing
beneath the silence
a balcony with lovers

The End

About the Author

John Karabetsos was born in Detroit, Michigan in 1972—the son of an English Professor and the second oldest of five brothers. Early on, he was drawn to narrative art: first in photography, then later at the University of Michigan in Ann Arbor, where he studied literature and theater.

As Karabetsos was completing his studies in Ann Arbor, his mentor Trianos Giagos, Professor of Papyrology and Greek, encouraged him to search deeper into the artistic consciousness of Western culture—and to do so specifically in Greece. He thus enrolled at Arcadia University in Athens, Greece in 1994. Later that year, Karabetsos retreated to the island of Santorini and composed the present collection, *Santorini Poems*, the first significant work of his career.

Since then, Karabetsos has continued to explore Western culture in a variety of media, always stressing commonality rather than difference. His photography has been exhibited at galleries in Dublin, Detroit, and Cleveland. He is a published journalist and member of the North American Snowsports Journalists Association, having produced articles on the Olympics as well as providing live correspondence for Detroit Public Radio, WRCJ during the 2006 Winter Olympics. More recently, Karabetsos has been focusing on performance art. He directed a feature film in Port Laoise, Ireland titled, *Vincent van Gogh: 70 Days in Laoise*, due to be released in the spring of 2019. And he is currently at work on his play about the life of photographer Vivian Maier, which is scheduled for production in Chicago during the fall of 2019.

Addendum for Notes

notes

notes

CPSIA information can be obtained
at www.ICGtesting.com
Printed in the USA
BVHW061052030719
552552BV00004B/53/P